P9-BYN-637

Italian Without Words

Don Cangelosi and Joseph Delli Carpini

Meadowbrook Press

Distributed by Simon & Schuster
New York, NY

Library of Congress Cataloging-in-Publication Data
Cangelosi, Don.
Italian without words / Don Cangelosi and Joseph
Delli Carpini
p. cm.
In English and Italian.
1. Gesture—Italy. I. Delli Carpini, Joseph. II. Title.
P117.5.I8C36   1989   001.56—dc19   88-31820
ISBN: 0-88166-156-2

Edited by Bruce Lansky
Production Editor: Wendy Ann Williams
Art Director: Kelly Nugent
Assistant Art Director: Shelagh Geraghty
Production Manager: Pam Scheunemann
Photography: Joseph Delli Carpini and Irving Schild
Models: Don Cangelosi and Jean Cangelosi

Simon & Schuster Ordering #: 0-671-67743-8

Copyright © 1989 by Don Cangelosi and Joseph Delli
Carpini

All rights reserved. No part of this book may be
reproduced in any form without permission from
the publisher, except in the case of brief quotations
embodied in critical articles and reviews.

Published by Meadowbrook Press, 18318
Minnetonka Boulevard, Deephaven, MN 55391

BOOK TRADE DISTRIBUTION by Simon & Schuster,
a division of Simon and Schuster, Inc., 1230
Avenue of the Americas, New York, NY 10020.

92 93   5 6 7 8 9

Printed in the United States of America

Italian Without Words

Contents

Dedication

To our parents, without whom
this book could not have been made.

Preface

Italians have always been a highly animated people. Hand gestures and facial expressions have played a major role in Italian interpersonal communication.

Through a variety of motions and body language Italians silently express their reactions to people and money, food and drink, pleasure and displeasure. By raising an eyebrow or opening a hand, anyone could convey threat, insult, or heartfelt love. But with each passing generation, these signs of yesterday slowly fade and are forgotten.

We hope this book will express and record our memories of yesterday in a humorous way. We do not intend to ridicule, embarrass, or demean the Italian people but rather to hold on to a part of our heritage and culture as a link to the past.

Don Cangelosi
Joseph Delli Carpini

Greetings, Goodbyes, Etc.

Hi!

Ciao!
(chow)

How're you doing?

Come stai?
(KOH-may sty)

I've got to go now.

Me ne devo andare adesso.
(may nay DAY-voh ahn-DAH-ray ah-DEH-soh)

It's been a pleasure.

È stato un piacere.
(eh STAH-toh oon PEE-ah-chay-ray)

Goodbye!

Arrivederci!
(ah-ree-vay-DAYR-chee)

Questions

What is it?

Che cosa è?
(kay KOH-zah eh)

What are you saying?
Che dice?
(kay DEE-chay)

What are you doing?
Che fai?
(kay FY)

What do you want?

Che vuoi?
(kay VWOY)

11

Are you kidding?

Stai scherzando?
(sty skehr-ZAHN-doh)

What can I do?

Che posso fare?
(kay PAH-soh FAH-ray)

13

Why me?
Perche me?
(pehr-KEH may)

What do I care?

Che me ne fotto?
(kay MAY nay FOH-toh)

What do you take me for... a fool?

Che pensi...sono un buffone?
(kay PEHN-see...soh-noh oon boof-OH-nay)

Common
Expressions

Listen to me!

Sentimi!
(SEHN-tee-mee)

I don't understand!

Non lo capisco!
(nohn loh kah-PEE-skoh)

I forgot!

Ho dimenticato!
(oh dee-mehn-tee-KAH-toh)

Help me, please!

Aiutami, per favore!
(ay-OO-tah-mee payr fah-VOH-ray)

Don't worry about it!

Non ti preoccupare!
(nohn tee pray-oh-koo-PAH-ray)

So, so.

Così-così.
(koh-ZEE koh-ZEE)

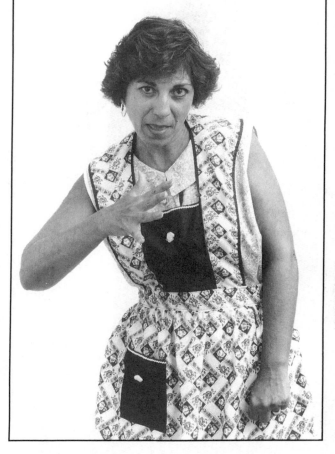

OK.

Va bene.
(vah BAY-nay)

We won!

Abbiamo vinto!
(ahb-YAH-moh VEEN-toh)

Insults

You're nuts!

Sei pazzo!
(SAY-ee PAHT-zoh)

You're a jerk!

Sei un citrullo!
(SAY-ee oon chee-TROO-loh)

You've got to be crazy!
Devi essere pazzo!
(DAY-vee EH-say-ray PAHT-zoh)

You've got a thick head!

Sei una testa dura!
(SAY-ee oo-nah TEH-stah DOO-rah)

You're a brownnoser.

Sei un leccapiedi.
(SAY-ee oon lay-kah-pee-EH-dee)

You dance like a fool.

Balli come uno scemo.
(BAH-lee KOH-may OON-oh SHAY-moh)

You're not worth spit!

Non vali una lira!
(nohn VAH-lee OO-nah LEE-rah)

You're a hoodlum!

Sei un malandrino!
(SAY-ee oon ma-lahn-DREE-noh)

You're a disgrace!

Disgraziato!
(deez-GRAHT-zee-ah-toh)

Go take a good shit! You'll feel a lot better.

Va' a fare una bella cacata! Ti sentirai meglio.
(vah ah FAH-ray OON-ah BEH-lah
kah-KAH-tah.
Tee SEHN-tee-RY-ee MEHL-yoh)

Mind your own business!

Fatti i fatti tuoi!
(FAH-tee ee FAH-tee TOY-ee)

You stink!

Tu puzzi!
(too POOT-zee)

The hell with you!

Va' al diavolo!
(vah ahl dee-AH-voh-loh)

Go to Hell! (The Horns)

Va' all' inferno!
(vah ahl een-FEHR-noh)

Damn you!

Mannaggia a te!
(mah-NAH-jah ah tay)

Up yours!
Va fa'n culo!
(vah fahn KOO-loh)

Now, get lost!
Ora, vattene!
(OH-rah VAH-tay-nay)

43

He was a good man.

Era un buon uomo.
(EH-rah oon bwohn WOH-moh)

Threats

Get over here now!

Vieni qui adesso!
(vee-YEHN-nee koo-ee ah-DEH-soh)

I'm warning you!

Ti sto avvertendo!
(tee stoh ah-vehr-TEHN-doh)

Wanna make something of it?

Vuoi farne qualcosa?
(vwoy FAHR-nay kwahl-KOH-sah)

I dare you!

Ti sfido. Provaci!
(tee SFEE-doh proh-VAH-chee)

Keep your mouth shut!
Stà zitto!
(STAH ZEE-toh)

I'll be watching you!

Ti tengo d'occhio!
(tee TEHN-goh DOH-kee-oh)

I'll put the evil eye on you.

Ti faccio il malocchio.
(tee fah-CHOH eel mahl-OCH-kee-oh)

Don't get me mad!

Non farmi arrabiare!
(nohn fahr-mee ah-rah-bee-AH-ray)

I'll smack you in the face!

Ti do uno schiaffo in faccia!
(tee doh OO-noh skee-YAH-foh een
FAH-chah)

I'll break your knees!

Ti rompo le ginocchia!
(tee RUM-poh lay jee-NOH-kee-yah)

I'll break your legs!

Ti rompo le gambe!
(tee RUM-poh lay GAHM-bay)

I'll blind you!

T'acceco!
(tah CHEH-koh)

I'll choke you!

Ti strangolo!
(tee strahn-GOH-loh)

I'll twist your neck!

Ti torco il collo!
(tee TOHR-koh eel KOH-loh)

I'll slit your throat!

Ti scanno!
(tee SKAH-noh)

Food and Drink

I'm hungry!
Ho fame!
(oh FAH-may)

Just a little bit!

Solo un po'!
(SOH-loh oon-poh)

It's too hot!
È troppo caldo!
(eh TROH-poh KAHL-doh)

Don't tell me how to cook!

Non mi dire come devo cucinare!
(nohn mee DEE-ray KOH-may DAY-voh
koo-chee-NAH-ray)

Get out of my kitchen!
Esci dalla mia cucina!
(EH-shee DAH-lah MEE-ah koo-CHEE-nah)

Hey, wait a minute!

Aspetta uno minuto!
(ah-SPEH-tah OO-noh mee-NOO-toh)

It's delicious!

È delizioso!
(eh day-leez-ee-OH-soh)

Let's have a drink!

Facciamoci un bicchiere!
(fah-CHAH-moh-chee oon bee-kee-AY-ray)

Cheers, to a hundred years!

Salute, a cent' anni!
(sah-LOO-tay, ah chehnt AHN-nee)

The check please.

Il conto per favore.
(eel KOHN-toh payr fah-VOH-ray)

I ate like a pig!

Ho mangiato come un porco!
(ho mahn-JAH-toh KOH-may oon POR-koh)

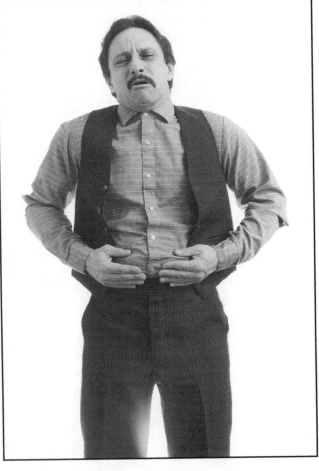

Men, Women
and Love

What a beautiful woman!

Che bella donna!
(kay BEHL-ah DOH-nah)

Are you talking to me?

Stai parlando con me?
(sty pahr-LAHN-doh kohn may)

You're beautiful!
Sei bella!
(SAY-ee BEH-lah)

What a hunk!

Che bel pezzo d'uomo!
(kay behl PEHT-zoh doo-OH-moh)

Come here, my dear.

Cara mia, vieni qui.
(KAH-rah MEE-ah, vee-YEH-nee koo-ee)

Let's have some fun!

Divertiamoci!
(dee-vehr-tee-AH-moh-chee)

You want to what?

Vuoi fare che cosa?
(vwoy FAH-ray kay KOH-zah)

You've got to be kidding!

Stai scherzando!
(sty skehr-ZAHN-doh)

Slow down.

Piano, piano.
(PYAH-noh PYAH-noh)

Enough is enough!

Adesso basta!
(ah-DEH-soh BAH-stah)

I've got a headache.

Mi fa male la testa.
(mee fah MAH-lay lah TEHS-tah)

Don't you dare touch me!

Non mi toccare!
(nohn mee toh-KAH-ray)

Come on, don't get mad.

Via, non t'arrabbiare.
(VEE-ah nohn tee-ah-rah-bee-YAH-ray)

You're making me crazy!
Mi fai impazzire!
(mee FY-ee eem-pah-ZEE-ray)

Don't leave me, I love you!

Non lasciarmi, ti voglio bene!
(nohn LAH-shar-mee, tee VOHL-yoh BEH-nay)

What will I tell my mother?

Che dirò a mia madre?
(kay DEE-roh ah MEE-ah MAH-dray)

Money

I'm broke!

Sono al verde!
(soh-noh ahl VEHR-day)

I don't have a penny!

Non ho un centesimo!
(nohn oh oon chehn-TEHS-ee-moh)

Look...my pockets are empty.

Guarda...ho le tasche vuote.
(GWAHR-dah oh lay TAH-skay VWOH-tay)

Don't get mad...I'll pay you.

Non t'arrabbiare...ti pagherò.
(nohn tee-ah-rah-bee-AH-ray...tee
pah-geh-ROH)

The deal stinks.

L'affare puzza.
(lah-FAH-ray POOT-zah)

English Index

Italian Index

Mother Murphy's Law
by Bruce Lansky

The wit of Bombeck and the wisdom of Murphy are combined in this collection of 325 laws that detail the perils and pitfalls of parenthood. Cartoon illustrations by Christine Tripp.

Order #1149

Mother Murphy's 2nd Law
by Bruce Lansky

A ribald collection of laws about love, sex, marriage and other skirmishes in the battle of the sexes. Mother Murphy offers rib-tickling advice to singles, marrieds and the divorced that they won't find in marriage and sex manuals.

Order #4010

Papal Bull
by Dean Sullivan
Illustrated by Pete Bastiansen

This witty dictionary contains definitions of over 500 words and expressions that every catholic hears and gives them new meanings.

Order #4060

Playing Fast and Loose with Time and Space
by P.S. Mueller

Here are 101 zany and off-beat cartoons that will appeal to fans of Mueller's nationally syndicated cartoon—and are sure to attract many more.

Order #4100

The Modern Girl's Guide to Everything
by Kaz Cooke

Hermoine, the Modern Girl, is the heroine of one of Australia's funniest and most successful syndicated comic strips. She's got advice for every single woman over the age of 18 on just about everything. She tells women how to find their lost innocence, use chocolate as a dieting aid, invest $68.10, and use PMS as a legal defense in any homicide. Her drawings are as hilarious as her advice.

Order #4090

Grandma Knows Best, But No One Ever Listens!
by Mary McBride

Mary McBride offers much-needed advice for new grandmas on how to:

- Show baby photos to anyone at any time.
- Get out of babysitting . . . or if stuck, to housebreak the kids before they wreck the house.
- Advise the daughter-in-law without being banned from her home. This is the perfect gift for Grandma. Phyllis Diller says it's "harder to put down than a new grandchild."

Order #4009

Grandma Knows Best Coffee Mug
The sequel to Mary McBride's best-selling book is a coffee mug. This high-quality ceramic mug makes an ideal gift for Grandma.

Order #3399

Order Form

Qty.	Title	Author	Order No.	Unit Cost	Total
	Best European Travel Tips	Whitman, J.	5070	$8.00	
	Dads Say the Dumbest Things!	Lansky/Jones	4220	$6.00	
	European Customs & Manners	Braganti/Devine	5080	$8.00	
	Grandma Knows Best	McBride, M.	4009	$5.00	
	Grandma Knows Best Mug	McBride, M.	3339	$5.00	
	How to Survive Your 40th Birthday	Dodds, B.	4260	$6.00	
	Italian Without Words	Cangelosi/Carpini	5100	$4.95	
	Modern Girl's Guide to Everything	Cooke, K.	4090	$4.95	
	Moms Say the Funniest Things!	Lansky, B.	4280	$6.00	
	Mother Murphy's Law	Lansky, B.	1149	$4.50	
	Mother Murphy's 2nd Law	Lansky, B.	4010	$4.50	
	Papal Bull	Sullivan, D.	4060	$4.95	
	Playing Fast & Loose with Time & Space	Mueller, P.	4100	$4.95	
	Prof. Pinkerton's Perplexing Puzzles	Maslanka, C.	6070	$4.95	
	Webster's Dictionary Game	Webster, W.	6030	$5.95	
				Subtotal	
		Shipping and Handling (see below)			
		MN residents add 6.5% sales tax			
				Total	

YES, please send me the books indicated above. Add $1.50 shipping and handling for the first book and $.50 for each additional book. Add $2.00 to total for books shipped to Canada. Overseas postage will be billed. Allow up to 4 weeks for delivery. Send check or money order payable to Meadowbrook Press. No cash or C.O.D.'s please. Prices subject to change without notice. **Quantity discounts available upon request.**

Send book(s) to:

Name _____

Address _____

City _____ State _____ Zip _____

Telephone (_____) _____

Payment via:

☐ Check or money order payable to Meadowbrook (No cash or C.O.D. please.)
  Amount enclosed $_____

☐ Visa (for orders over $10.00 only.) ☐ MasterCard (for orders over $10.00 only.)
Account #_____

Signature _____ Exp. Date _____

A *FREE* Meadowbrook Press catalog is available upon request.
You can also phone us for orders of $10.00 or more at 1-800-338-2232.

Mail to:
Meadowbrook, Inc.
18318 Minnetonka Boulevard, Deephaven, Minnesota 55391
(612) 473-5400   Toll-Free 1-800-338-2232   Fax (612) 475-0736